1. Whilst we have made every effort to achieve accuracy in the preparation of material for this guide book, the author, publisher and copyright owners can take no responsibility for trespass, irresponsible riding, any loss or damage to persons or property suffered as a result of the route descriptions or advice in this book.

2. All rights reserved.
No part of this publication may be reproduced, stored in a retrieval system, or transmitted in any form or by any means, electronic, mechanical, photocopied, recording or otherwise, without the prior permission of the Publisher and the copyright holder.

3. All text copyright Gillian Rowan-Wilde. The contents of this publication are believed correct at the time of printing. Nevertheless, the Publishers cannot accept responsibility for errors and omissions, or for changes in details given.

Wilde's Leisure Guides are a trade mark of Gildersleve Publishing Ltd.

© Copyright Gillian Rowan-Wilde

Published by
Gildersleve Publishing Ltd
Capricorn House, Blackburn Road
Rising Bridge, Lancashire BB5 2AA

ACKNOWLEDGMENTS
To the Access Officers for Dartmoor and Exmoor National Parks and the Public Rights of Way Officers for both Devon and Cornwall, for their help and advice in their specific areas.

Last but not least the originators of all the trails without which it would have been impossible to start this journey.

Maps based upon Ordinance Survey mapping with the permission of the Controller of Her Majesty's Stationery, Office,
© Crown copyright 84393M.

GENERAL INFORMATION

THE OFFROAD CYCLING CODE

STAY ON THE TRAIL
Only ride bridleways & byways
Avoid footpaths
Plan your route in advance
GIVE WAY TO HORSES & WALKERS
Make sure you are heard when riding up behind anyone
Ride Carefully, keep to the left of anyone approaching you.
NEVER RIDE IN LARGE GROUPS
5 or 6 is maximum
BE KIND TO BIRDS, ANIMALS & PLANTS
Keep your dog under control
PREVENT EROSION
Avoid skidding and locking your wheels when braking.
CLOSE GATES BEHIND YOU
Don't climb walls or force hedges
EQUIPMENT FOR SAFETY
Wear a helmet
Take a first aid kit
Carry enough food and drink
Pack waterproofs & warm clothes
Take essential spares & tools
TAKE PRIDE IN YOUR BIKE
Maintain your bike before you leave, and on your return.
BE TIDY
Take all your litter home
Never create a fire hazard
ENJOY YOUR CYCLING
Try not to get annoyed with anyone, it never solves a problem Don't make unnecessary noise

RIGHTS OF WAY

Off-road cyclists have right of way on most public bridleways and other tracks unless forbidden by a bye-law. You must give way to walkers and horseriders.

By-ways, which are usually unsurfaced tracks are open to cyclists, as well as walkers and horseriders, you may also find vehicles have right to access.

There is NO right of way on Public Footpaths, if cyclists finds themselves on a public footpath they must get off their bike and walk.

A cyclist is NOT permitted to ride his bike on the pavements.

On moorland, upland or farmland a cyclist normally has NO right of access without the express permission of the landowner.

Tow-paths by the canals normally require a permit from the appropriate British Waterways.

There are quite a few designated cycle routes and paths to be found in urban areas, on Waterways tow-paths, Forestry Commission land or on disused railway lines.

Cyclists must adhere to the Highway Code.

GENERAL SAFETY HINTS

1. Make sure your bike is safe to ride befor_____ to take with _____re inner_____ s and lever_____
forge_____
2. Yo_____ lights after_____
3. Al_____ ident_____
4. Al_____ going _____
5. Le_____ id and take _____
6. W_____ othes, better_____
7. Ri_____ wn hill, _____
8. It is adviseable to always wear a helmet.
9. Carry a water bottle, always keep it filled especially on a hot day. Take spare food, drink and clothing with you.
10. Be very careful when riding on marsh land or scree especially when it is wet.
11. Always take a detailed map with you for adventurous or wilderness trips. Have a compass with you. Take a whistle with you to use when calling for help should you have an accident.
12. Always be aware of others using the same path as yourself. They also want to enjoy their day out!
13. General maintenance of your bike on your return home. Making sure it is cleaned and oiled ready for your next trip.

PACKING YOUR ESSENTIALS

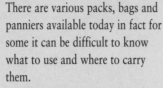

There are various packs, bags and panniers available today in fact for some it can be difficult to know what to use and where to carry them.

Illustrated are a number of carrying positions for different capacities of bags. In addition to these there are a variety of touring front and rear panniers available. Coming from a walking background I prefer to use a small daysac in which I carry my food and waterproofs with a bar bag on the bike which usually has my tool kit, chocolate, maps and camera. Other people I know prefer to keep their body free and carry everything on their bikes - so you should do which ever feels comfortable.

Bar Bag • Bum Bag • Rucksack

Bar Bag • Rack Pack

Stem Bag • Wedge Bag • Seat Bag

CONTENTS

PACKING YOUR ESSENTIALS	4
TRAIL LOCATION MAP - KEY	5
PLYM VALLEY TRAIL	6
EGGESFORD	8
GT. HALDEN & BULLER'S HILL	9
TARKA TRAIL Barnstaple-Gt.Torrington	10
TARKA TRAIL Gt.Torrington-Petrockstowe	12
BURRATOR RESERVOIR	14
BOVEY VALLEY & EASDON TOR	16
OKEHAMPTON Hangstone Hill	18
POSTBRIDGE Bellever Forest & Soussons Down	20
CASTLE DROGO	22
ILFRACOMBE - MORTEHOE	23
PRINCETOWN Tyrwhitt Cycleway	24
BARNSTAPLE - BRAUNTON BURROWS	25
PORTREATH TRAMWAY & Tehidy Country Park	28
PENTEWAN VALLEY	30
CARDINHAM WOODS	31
THE CAMEL TRAIL Padstow-Wadebridge	32
THE CAMEL TRAIL Wadebridge-Poley's Bridge	34
BRENDON COMMON 'Doone Country'	36
DUNSTER PARK & CROYDON HILL	38
BRIDGWATER & TAUNTON CANAL	40
QUANTOCK HILLS	42
TOTNES - DARTINGTON HALL	44
EXETER Ship Canal	45
CYCLE HIRE	46
ACCOMMODATION GUIDE	47-48
YOUTH HOSTELS	49
TOURIST INFORMATION CENTRES 🛈	50
LIFE EDUCATION CENTRES	51-52

WILDE'S
LEISURE GUIDES

CYCLE ROUTE GUIDE
TO 30 LEISURE TRAILS

DEVON, CORNWALL AND
WEST SOMERSET

Written by
Gillian Rowan-Wilde

Published by
GILDERSLEVE
PUBLISHING LIMITED

ABOUT THE AUTHOR

Gillian Rowan-Wilde took up leisure cycling in the summer of 1993, her first trail being the Tarka Trail which she undertook during a holiday in Devon. Since then she has ridden over 200 trails.

As well as cycling she is an accomplished fell and mountain walker. Among her accomplishments as a walker, are the completion of one of the '100' mile walks, Mountain Marathons and numerous challenge walks over 30 miles.

She has completed courses at Glencoe in Scotland on rock and ice climbing also survival techniques whilst on the mountains with instructors from the Crowden Outdoor Pursuits Centre.

In this series of guides she hopes to bring to the leisure cyclist a catalogue of historical and interesting features on rides, together with some of the wildlife you may encounter.

MAPS BY

Andy Thelwell has grown up with Apple Macs and computer graphics. At present he is employed as a technical manager with a leading north west art studio

In his spare time he is either in the gym, or out off-road on his mountain bike.

ILLUSTRATION BY

Graham Nicholson studied illustration at Lincoln, since then he has been commissioned by many leading national, and international companies, supplying work for packaging, advertising campaign's and corporate brochures.

In his leisure time he is a keen walker, an interest he shares with his family.

INTRODUCTION

In the last four years Gillian and I have ridden over 200 off road routes and with the publishing of this , our fourth book, 110 of these routes are now in print covering some of the most varied and beautiful scenery in England.

We started this book in Summer '93 and have spent our summer holidays since then compiling this selection of rides. During this time we have experienced many magical moments from the tranquillity of riding the upper parts of the Tarka and Camel trails to the moods and breathtaking views over Dartmoor and Exmoor.

This book like our others, gives a selection of various routes, some are challenging but the majority are through undulating country. There are rides in forests over moors following rivers and canals. Most of our recommended rides are on trails with reasonable surfaces with the exception of the moorland routes and we would advise not to undertake these in wet weather.

Each route has its own custom drawn map showing everything you need to know from distances and directions to parking, picnic and rest stops.

As far as I am aware we are the only company producing off road cycle routes that have the routes vetted by the relevant countryside access officers. These custodians of our environment are most helpful and ask us to be mindful of the potential impact we can have on the flora and fauna on these trails particularly in wet conditions where a large number of users can cause erosion. In forestry areas routes may be changed to allow forestry working. In these instances take the signed detours or check with the on site forestry information centres.

As with our last book we have included an accommodation listing for these who may want to stay over together with a list of cycle hire centres for people who need to hire.

We hope that you enjoy riding the routes in this book as much as we have in riding and compiling them.

Happy cycling *Peter*

KEY

i Information Centre

P Parking

PC Public Convenience

☎ Telephone

⛉ Picnic Area

⛺ Camp Site

  Caravan Site

  Public House/Hotel

⛵ Boating

✝ Church

  Mill

  Built up Area

  Quarry

———— Cycle Trail
———— Main Road
———— Minor Road
- - - - - Footpath
·····•····· Railway Track
- - - - - National Park Boundary

  River/Stream

  Lake/Reservoir

  Mixed Wood

  Coniferous Wood

TRAIL LOCATION MAP

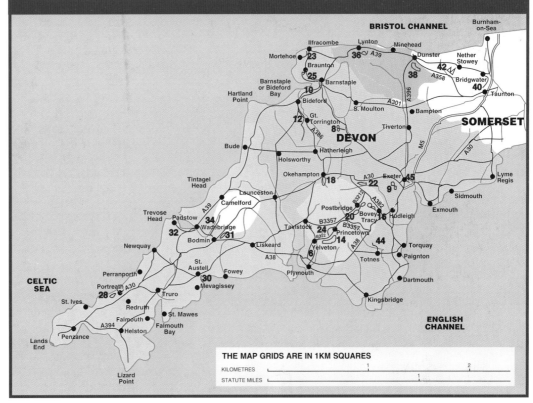

THE MAP GRIDS ARE IN 1KM SQUARES

KILOMETRES   1   2

STATUTE MILES   1

———— Trail (page Number)
Somerset   Exmoor National Park
Devon   Dartmoor National Park
Cornwall   Bodmin Moor

PLYM VALLEY TRAIL

THE PLYM VALLEY TRAIL IS SITUATED ON THE EAST BANK OF THE RIVER PLYM WITH THE A379 KINGSBRIDGE-PLYMOUTH ROAD TO THE SOUTH. THE CITY OF PLYMOUTH AND SALTASH TOWN LIE WEST OF THE TRAIL.

This trail follows the beautiful valley of the River Plym through woodland, over several viaducts used by the old railway line and finally onto the magnificent moorland of Dartmoor National Park.

In 1859 the railway line was part of the South Devon and Tavistock Railway which originally was overseen by the great engineer Brunel. Later became part of the old Great Western Railway line linking industry to the port of Plymouth.

There are four spectacular viaducts on this trail, Cann Viaduct is the first, then Riverford Viaduct built in 1893 stands 97ft high with five tall arches. The third and highest is Bickleigh Viaduct standing 123ft high with seven arches spanning the gorge - Brunel's original wooden structure can be seen below, and fourth is at Ham Green and the longest, looking across Bickleigh Vale and the high moors of Dartmoor.

From Point Cottage you can ride down to Laira Bridge to commence your trail or continue through the grounds of Saltram House, built in the 16th Century and now belonging to the National Trust. From the track you can see Plym Bridge spanning the river where in 1238 the first bridge was built

for the monastic centre at Plympton. For many years this bridge was the lowest crossing point of the River for anyone going into Plymouth.

Shaugh Tunnel is an impressive 308 yds long and follows the curve of the railway track making it impossible to see both the entrance and exit at one time.

sustrans

START : S		Car Park (Point Cottage) beside the grounds of Saltram House
FINISH :		Clearbrook
MAP :		O.S. Landranger 201 (Plymouth & Launceston)
LENGTH (approx) :		13 ¾ km (8 ½m) Linear
SURFACE :		Stone based grit/tarmac
RIDE RATING :		Easy Adventurous

NOTES : *A torch is required for Shaugh Tunnel*

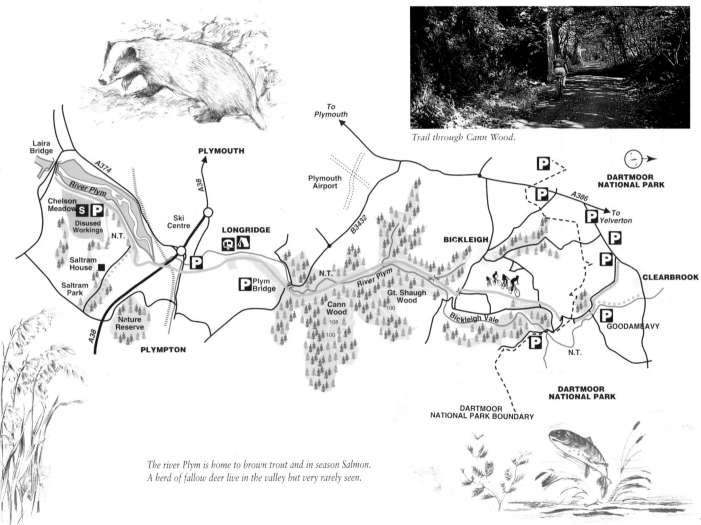

Laira
Bridge

PLYMOUTH

To
Plymouth

PLYMOUTH

A374

River Plym

Chelson
Meadow

S **P**

Disused
Workings

N.T.

Saltram
House

Saltram
Park

Nature
Reserve

A38

A38

Ski
Centre

P

LONGRIDGE

P Plym
Bridge

N.T.

Cann
Wood

108

100

Plymouth
Airport

B3432

River Plym

Gt. Shaugh
Wood

100

Trail through Cann Wood.

P

P

A386

P To
Yelverton

P

**DARTMOOR
NATIONAL PARK**

BICKLEIGH

P

CLEARBROOK

Bickleigh Vale

P

P

GOODAMEAVY

N.T.

P

PLYMPTON

DARTMOOR
NATIONAL PARK BOUNDARY

**DARTMOOR
NATIONAL PARK**

*The river Plym is home to brown trout and in season Salmon.
A herd of fallow deer live in the valley but very rarely seen.*

7

EGGESFORD
Heywood and Flashdown woods

THESE WOODS ARE SITUATION ON THE A377 BARNSTAPLE TO CREDITON ROAD SOUTH OF CHULMLEIGH AND NORTH OF COPPLESTONE. THE TURNING FOR THE TRAIL IS OVER THE LEVEL CROSSING BESIDE EGGESFORD STATION ON THE A377.

Eggesford is managed by the Forestry Commision and the valley of the River Taw provides a habitate for a large variety of wild animals and the Buzzards who circle and soar around the tree tops of the forest.

Flashdown wood has an excellent signposted trail returning to the road at the top of the hill. For the route through Heywood Woods turn left at the road and right at the cross roads, pass the entrance to the Wembworthy Centre and follow the signposted trail through the woods. At the most northerly point of Heywood wood there is a mound with the remains of a Norman bailey castle. On your return path through the woods there are three very unusual trees - an enormously tall Douglas fir, a wide monkey puzzle tree (Chilean Pine) and a vast Western Red Cedar.

START & FINISH :	**S**	Eggesford Country Centre
MAP :		O.S. Landranger 180 (Barnstaple) and 191 (Okehampton)
LENGTH (approx) :		11km (7m) Circular
SURFACE :		Forest tracks/tarmac/gravel
RIDE RATING :		Moderate Adventurous

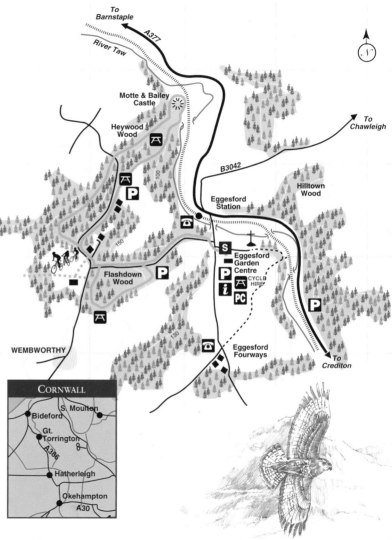

8

GREAT HALDEN & BULLER'S HILL

THESE WOODS ARE SITUATED SOUTH/WEST OF EXETER. NORTH AND WEST OF THE A38 EXETER-PLYMOUTH ROAD AND HALDON RACE COURSE.

Excellent forest trails with some exciting hills both down and UP! Through the forest follow paths with the horseshoe signs.

For the start of route 1 - ‒‒‒‒ Turn right on to the road out of the (picnic site) then left through a gate marked 'riding by permit only' into the forest. Follow the bridleway signposts through the forest taking care as roads are crossed.

Starting route 2 - ▬▬ Turn right on to the road past the Forestry Commission car park onto a cut-through. Turn right and immediately left onto a gated track into the forest (ignore the surfaced track on your left).

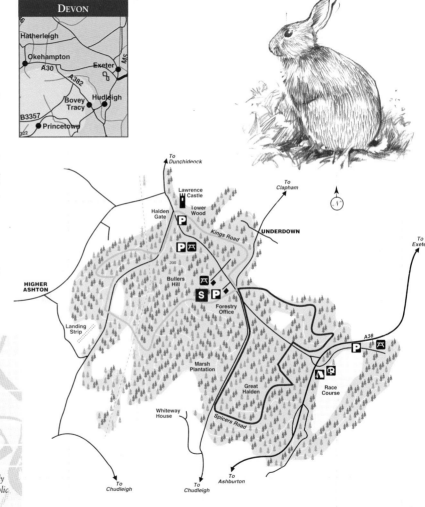

START & FINISH 1 &2 : 🅂	Buller's Hill Car Park (Picnic site)
MAP :	O.S. Landranger 191 (Okehampton) 192 (Exeter, Sidmouth)
LENGTH (approx) :	Route 1 7km(4 ½m) Circular Route 2 7km (4 ½m) Circular
SURFACE :	Forest tracks/tarmac
RIDE RATING :	Both routes - Moderate Adventurous

NOTES : Care must be taken to stay on the bridlepaths when going through the privately owned woodland. Do NOT cycle on any of the tracks marked 'retained shooting no public access'.

9

TARKA TRAIL
Barnstaple - Great Torrington

THE TARKA TRAIL IS SITUATED NORTH OF THE DARTMOOR NATIONAL PARK AND SOUTH BARNSTAPLE AND THE TAW ESTUARY. EAST OF THE RIVER TORRIDGE BUT WEST OF THE RIVER TAW.

The Tarka country offers a stunning range of spectacular scenery along the broad expanse of the Rivers Taw and Torridge. The route should be explored in its entirety to understand the full beauty of this trail which follows the bed of the old railway line.

The Tarka trail starts from Barnstaple railway station car park. Follow the well marked blue arrow signposts with an otter footprint superimposed on it out of the station yard along the cycle track towards Bideford south of the River Taw.

There are various access points along the route but the track beside the estuary of the Taw is one not to be missed. The wild flowers are in abundance also the various sea birds can be watched on the Isley March RSPB reserve. Follow the trail over the road at Instow passing through the old railway station and signalbox to East-the-Water and Bideford where there is a carriage at the old station, now an information centre.

The steep wooded sides of the valley in the 'land of two rivers' inspired Henry Williamson to write the book 'Tarka the Otter' and although the book was written in the 1920's the landscape has not changed a great deal since then.

Old Railway Station, Instow.

START :	S	Barnstaple Railway Station
FINISH :		Great Torrington
MAP :		O.S. Landranger 180 (Barnstaple & Ilfracombe area)
LENGTH (approx) :		28km (17m) Linear
SURFACE :		Tarmac/gravel/sand
RIDE RATING :		Easy

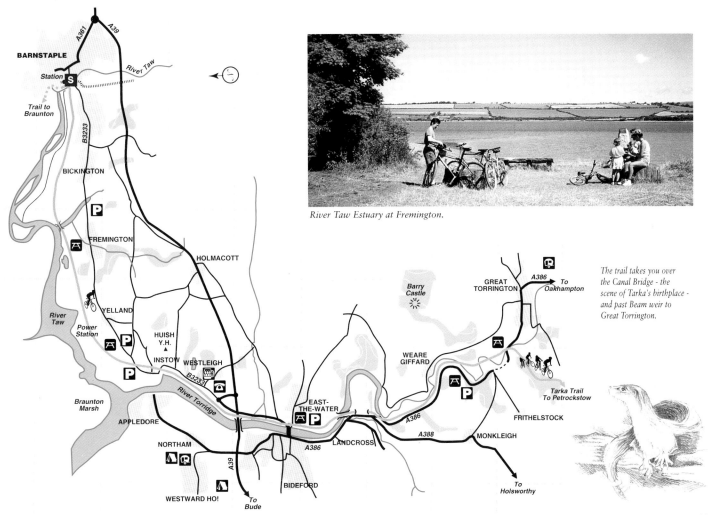

BARNSTAPLE

Station **S**

Trail to Braunton

River Taw

A361 A39

B3233

BICKINGTON

P

FREMINGTON

HOLMACOTT

River Taw

Power Station

YELLAND

P

HUISH Y.H. ▲

INSTOW

WESTLEIGH

B3233

River Torridge

Braunton Marsh

P

APPLEDORE

NORTHAM

A39

WESTWARD HO!

To Bude

BIDEFORD

EAST-THE-WATER

P

LANDCROSS

A386

A386

A388

MONKLEIGH

To Holsworthy

Barry Castle

WEARE GIFFARD

P

GREAT TORRINGTON

A386

To Oakhampton

P

FRITHELSTOCK

Tarka Trail To Petrockstow

River Taw Estuary at Fremington.

The trail takes you over the Canal Bridge - the scene of Tarka's birthplace - and past Beam weir to Great Torrington.

11

TARKA TRAIL
Great Torrington - Petrockstowe

THIS TRAIL IS SITUATED WEST OF THE RIVER TORRIDGE AND EAST OF THE A388
BIDEFORD-HOLSWORTHY ROAD.

The southern section of the Tarka Trail is along the old track bed of the
disused railway line that used to bring the clay from Petrockstowe quarries
to Bideford through beautiful wooded areas and open countryside.

The trail takes its name from one of the best known animal
stories 'Tarka the Otter' published in 1927. The countryside
around the River Torridge has changed very little except for
the demise of the North Devon Railway and the line's
closure in 1965.

The Tarka trail is indicated by signposts with a blue arrow
and an otter footprint superimposed. From the old Torrington
station the trail crosses over the River Torridge on a 700ft viaduct and
follows one of the tributaries of the Torridge. The trail from
the viaduct goes slightly uphill through the woodland section, a much
appreciated descent back to Torrington at the end of the day.

A couple of the old platforms belonging to the old North Devon railway
can still be seen along the trail which is a reminder of the days when
clay quarried near Petrockstowe would be taken by rail to the ships
lying along the quayside in Bideford.

Trail along the old railway line track bed near East Yarde.

START :	**S**	Old railway station Torrington (Puffing Billy pub on the A386)
FINISH :		Petrockstowe
MAP :		O.S. Landranger 180 (Barnstaple) Landranger 191 (Okehampton)
LENGTH (approx) :		14 km (8 ½ m) Linear
SURFACE :		Grass/hard grit
RIDE RATING :		Easy Adventurous

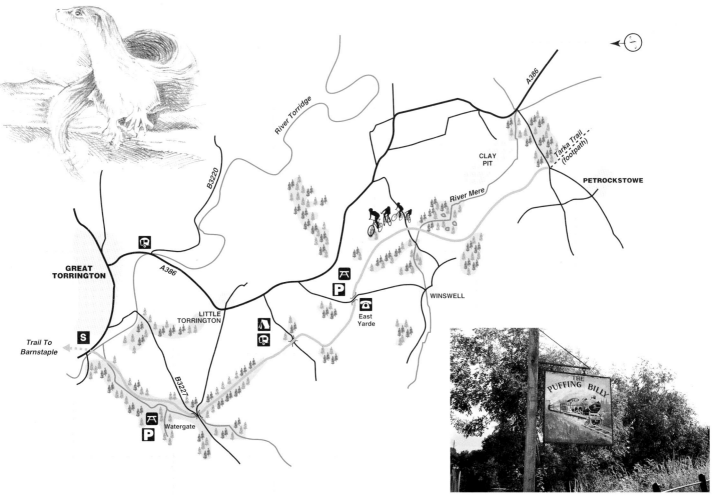

River Torridge

B3220

CLAY PIT

River Mere

A386

Tarka Trail (footpath)

PETROCKSTOWE

GREAT TORRINGTON

A386

LITTLE TORRINGTON

WINSWELL

East Yarde

Trail To Barnstaple

B3227

Watergate

'Puffing Billy' at Gt. Torrington old railway station.

BURRATOR RESERVOIR
The 'Tor and Cross' Trail

Burrator Reservoir.

THIS TRAIL IS SITUATION EAST OF YELVERTON AND THE A386 PLYMOUTH-OKEHAMPTON ROAD. TO THE NORTH IS THE B32112 FROM PRINCETOWN AND TO THE SOUTH IS THE RIVER PLYM.

This route epitomises Dartmoor National Park with its beautiful but barren moorland 'Tors' capped with rocks that look as though they are going to tumble off at any moment, and the mysterious legends that surround the 'crosses'.

The route begins on the lane beside Burrator Reservoir going towards the dam and the hamlet of Sheepstor. The road passes a country house hotel and a very

pretty church before ending in a small car park and a Ministry of Defence sign forbidding any vehicles past this point.
Follow the track over a ford and up the hill past a clump of trees and a scout hut on your right. Keep to the left hand track after Eylesbarrow's disused Tin Min crossing the top of the moors before going down the hill passing Nun's Cross. At the track cross roads, turn left to see the wonderful view of Burrator Reservoir stretched out in front of you.

START & FINISH :	S	Burrator Reservoir
MAP :		O.S. Outdoor Leisure 28 (Dartmoor) Landranger 202 (Torbay & S.Dartmoor)
LENGTH (approx) :		15km (9 ½ m) Circular
SURFACE :		Moorland paths/rough stone
RIDE RATING :		Hard

NOTES : *The mist can roll over the moorland very quickly, be sure the weather forecast is good before starting this route.*

Nuns Cross on Dartmoor looking across to Burrator Reservoir.

Leather Tor Bridge over the River Meavy.

Beware his track although cycleable, becomes steep and very stoney as it descends into the woods and over the bridge spanning the River Meavy. Climb up to the lane to "Cross Gate". Turn sharp left down the hill into the woods and back to the car park.

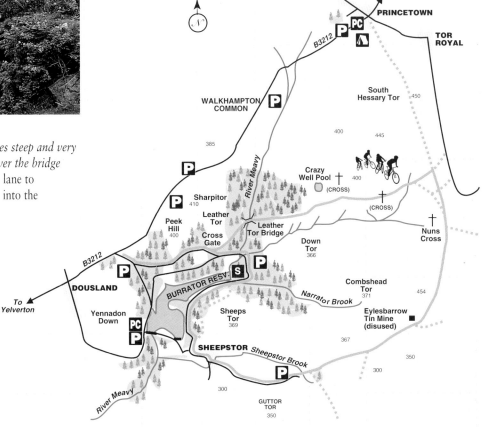

BOVEY VALLEY & EASDON TOR CIRCULAR

Becka Brook.

These two trails are situation west of the A382 Bovey Tracey-Moretonhampstead road and east of Hameldown Tor. North is North Bovey and south is the B3387 road to Widecombe-in-the-Moor.

Both routes have spectacular scenery, and panoramic views especially from the road section back to Bovey Tracey from Manaton. The beauty of Dartmoor National Park lies in the contrast between the open moorland around Easdon Tor and the wooded valley of the River Bovey.

The forest section on route 1 after the bridge over Becka Brook can be difficult to follow but as long as you keep on the main track up the hill through the woods and do not deviate left or right you will meet the path at the top. Bear right at this T-junction of paths and carry on up hill through the gate. At the road crossing turn right into the hamlet of Water signposted 'indirect route to Manaton'. Turn sharp left at the entrance beside the farmyard and continue on the track up the hill into Manaton.

START & FINISH :	S¹	(Route 1) A382 Road North of Bovey Tracy
	S²	(Route 2) Manaton
MAP :		O.S. Outdoor Leisure 28 (Dartmoor)
		Landranger 191 (Okehampton & N.Dartmoor)
LENGTH (approx) :		(Route 1) 17km (10 ½m) Circular
		(Route 2) 12km (8m) Circular
SURFACE :		(R.1-2) Tarmac/stoney (R.1) Forest tracks
RIDE RATING :		(Route 1) Hard
		(Route 2) Moderate Adventurous

NOTES : Route 1 - The ½ mile on the disused railway line. Cyclists are allowed to use this route by kind permission of the National Trust. Please ride carefully - many other users walk this path.

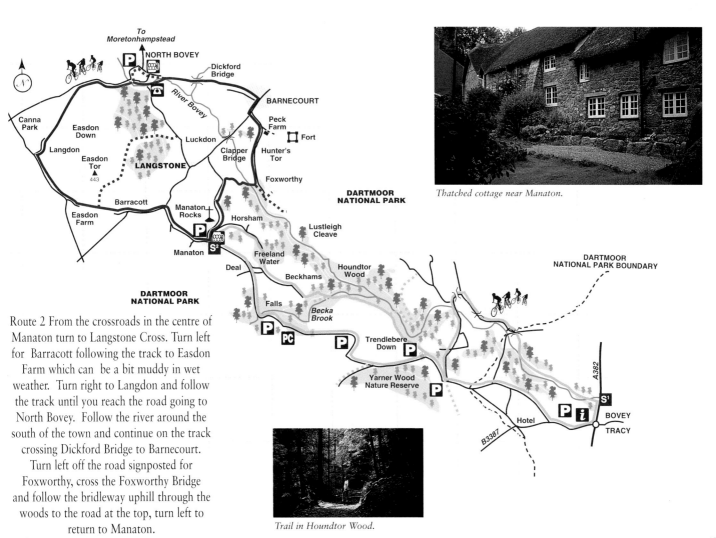

To Moretonhampstead

P **NORTH BOVEY**

Dickford Bridge

River Bovey

BARNECOURT

Canna Park

Easdon Down

Langdon

Easdon Tor ▲ 443

Luckdon

Peck Farm

□ Fort

Hunter's Tor

Clapper Bridge

LANGSTONE

Barracott

Easdon Farm

Manaton Rocks

P **S²**

Manaton

Horsham

Deal

Freeland Water

Beckhams

Falls

Becka Brook

P

PC

P

Foxworthy

DARTMOOR NATIONAL PARK

Lustleigh Cleave

Houndtor Wood

Trendlebere Down

P

Yarner Wood Nature Reserve

P

Hotel

B3387

A382

DARTMOOR NATIONAL PARK BOUNDARY

P **i** **S¹**

BOVEY TRACY

DARTMOOR NATIONAL PARK

Route 2 From the crossroads in the centre of Manaton turn to Langstone Cross. Turn left for Barracott following the track to Easdon Farm which can be a bit muddy in wet weather. Turn right to Langdon and follow the track until you reach the road going to North Bovey. Follow the river around the south of the town and continue on the track crossing Dickford Bridge to Barnecourt. Turn left off the road signposted for Foxworthy, cross the Foxworthy Bridge and follow the bridleway uphill through the woods to the road at the top, turn left to return to Manaton.

Thatched cottage near Manaton.

Trail in Houndtor Wood.

OKEHAMPTON
Hangingstone Hill

THIS TRAIL IS SITUATED SOUTH OF OKEHAMPTON AND THE A30 EXETER - LAUNCESTON ROAD. NORTH OF DARTMOOR FOREST AND WEST OF SOUTH ZEAL.

This Hangingstone Hill route is over the wide open barren moorland of Dartmoor National Park. The views over Dartmoor are wonderful as you climb up Okement Hill and look over Okehampton Common and Dartmoor Forest.

To start this trail to Hangingstone Hill take the road out of Okehampton towards Okehampton Camp. Turn left off this road towards the park and follow the bridleway signs through the park beside the river. Beside the

START & FINISH :	**S**	Okehampton
MAP :		O.S. Outdoor Leisure 28 (Dartmoor)
		Landranger 191 (Okehampton & N.Dartmoor)
LENGTH (approx) :		21km (13 m) Circular
SURFACE :		Tarmac/grass track
RIDE RATING :		Hard

arches of the railway bridge ford the river keeping to the north side of the railway and take the road up the hill following the bridleway signs. At the crossroads turn right for Belstone Village. Once in the hamlet of Belstone turn right at the crossroads following the bridleway signposts keeping the church and the Inn on your left.

Belstone Common.

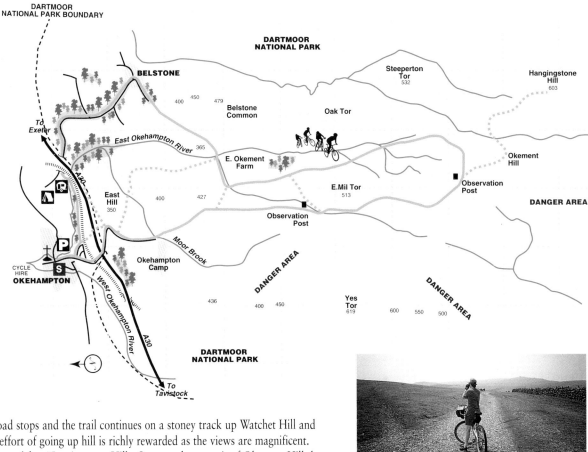

NOTES : This area of the National Park is widely used by the Ministry of Defence for training purposes. Access is available over most of the area but check the firing times in the local paper. When red flags are flying this is to warn the public the firing ranges are in use.

DARTMOOR NATIONAL PARK BOUNDARY

To Exeter

BELSTONE

DARTMOOR
NATIONAL PARK

Steeperton Tor
532

Hangingstone Hill
603

400 450 479

Belstone Common

Oak Tor

East Okehampton River

365

E. Okement Farm

Okement Hill

Observation Post

DANGER AREA

E.Mil Tor
513

East Hill
350

400 427

Observation Post

Moor Brook

Okehampton Camp

DANGER AREA

DANGER AREA

CYCLE HIRE
OKEHAMPTON

West Okehampton River

A30

436

400 450

Yes Tor
619

600 550 500

DARTMOOR
NATIONAL PARK

To Tavistock

Once up the hill the road stops and the trail continues on a stoney track up Watchet Hill and up onto the moor the effort of going up hill is richly rewarded as the views are magnificent. Follow the track signposted for Hangingstone Hill. Once on the summit of Okement Hill the return ride is an exhilarating 4 mile descent past Okehampton Camp back to Okehampton.

Stoney track on Watchet Hill above Belstone.

POSTBRIDGE

Bellever Forest & Soussons Down

<small>THESE TRAILS ARE SITUATED WEST OF THE B3213 PRINCETOWN TO MORTONHAMPSTEAD ROAD WITHIN THE DARTMOOR NATIONAL PARK. SOUTH OF THE FOREST IS THE WEST DART RIVER AND NORTH IS FENWORTHY FOREST.</small>

These trails are on excellent tracks within the forest and the paths are bridleway signposted. These is an abundance of wildlife within the forest, and many varieties of wild flowers which in places is like a carpet on the forest floor.

Route 1 - This trail begins in Postbridge car park over the road and into Bellever Forest. Turn right to follow one of the signposted trails through the forest, round past Bellever and Laughter Tor, along the path near East Dart River, either   descend the hill back towards Postbridge or   join the two routes by cycling past the Youth Hostel out of Bellever Forest, over Bellever Bridge, down the lane before turning left on to the bridleway over Cator Common to Soussons Down.

Route 2 - The trail for Soussons Down starts in the car park (opp. side of the road to the Inn). Follow the well defined track until a crossing of the paths. Take the right hand path (going south) into the forest. The permitted tracks through the wooded Down area are all indicated with bridleway signposts.

START & FINISH :		
S¹	(Route 1)	Postbridge Car Park
S²	(Route 2)	Car Park on the B3212

MAP : O.S. Outdoor Leisure 28 (Dartmoor)
Landranger 191 ((Okehampton & N.Dartmoor)

LENGTH (approx) : (Route 1) 9 km (5 m) Circular
(Route 2) 11 km (6 ⁷/₄km) Circular
Bridleway joining the two trails 5km (3m)

SURFACE : Forest tracks/Tarmac

RIDE RATING : Both routes : Moderate

Riding down to the Farm on Soussons Down.

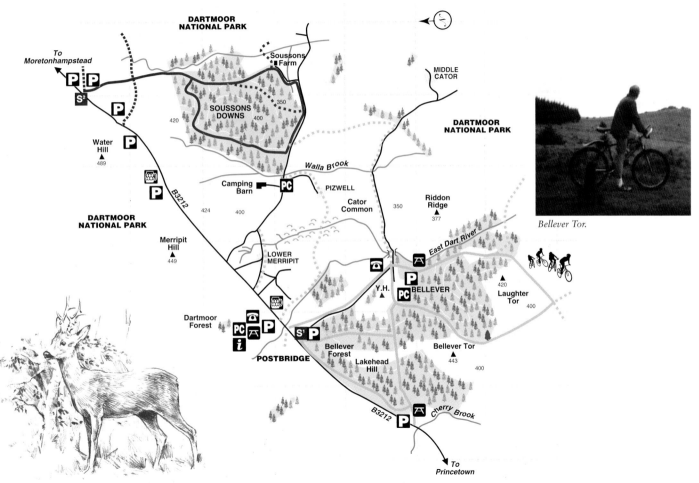

Bellever Tor.

CASTLE DROGO

THE TRAIL IS WITHIN THE DARTMOOR NATIONAL PARK. NORTH OF MORTONHAMPSTEAD AND EAST OF THE A382. SOUTH OF THE DREWSTEIGNTON AND THE A30 EXETER-OKEHAMPTON ROAD.

Castle Drogo was designed by Lutyens and built for Julius Drew in 1930. The grounds are magnificent with a beautiful circular croquet lawn (mallets for hire) and splendid views over the 300ft gorge down into the woods along the River Teign.

START & FINISH :	**S** Castle Drogo N.T. car park
MAP :	O.S. Outdoor Leisure 28 (Dartmoor) Landranger 191 (Okehampton & N.Dartmoor)
LENGTH (approx) :	8 km (5m) Circular
SURFACE :	Forest tracks/tarmac
RIDE RATING :	Moderate

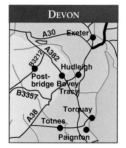

The trail starts from the castle grounds by turning left on to the road and left again on to the bridleway signposted to Fingle's Bridge. The path along the River Teign to Fingle's Bridge and the track through the woods to Drewsteignton make this a beautiful circular ride with an abundance of woodland plants and wildlife.

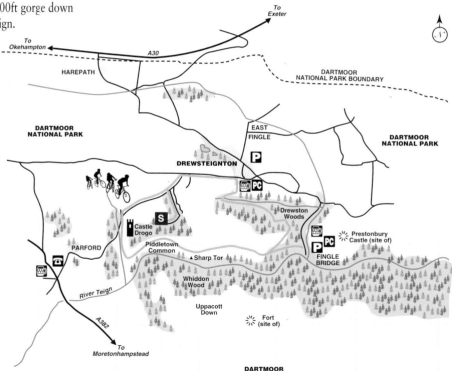

Castle Drogo.

THE NATIONAL TRUST

ILFRACOMBE - MORTEHOE

THIS TRAIL LIES WEST OF THE A361 ILFRACOMBE BRAUNTON ROAD WITH THE COASTAL PATH OVERLOOKING THE BRITISL CHANNEL TO THE NORTH AND WEST. THE B3343 TO WOOLACOMBE IS TO THE SOUTH.

START : **S**	Ilfracombe - Cairn Nature Reserve
FINISH :	Mortehoe
MAP :	O.S. Landranger 180 (Barnstaple & Ilfracombe)
LENGTH (approx) :	8km (5 m) Linear
SURFACE :	Stone based grit/tarmac
RIDE RATING :	Easy

NOTES : *Our trail starts at Cairn nature reserve due to the steep hill and steps out of Ilfracombe*

The first part of the trail from The Cairn Nature Reserve to Lee Bridge is along the bed of an old railway line which opened in 1874. Due to the 1 in 36 incline out of Ilfracombe two steam engines were frequently used, often having to return to the start to have a second attempt to pull the wagons up the hill. The narrow path is banked with wild plants with clouds of Red Admiral butterlies enjoying the blossoms through to late summer. The view looking across the Bristol Channel to Wales is excellent, as are the panoramic views of the hills to the west known as the 'Tors'.

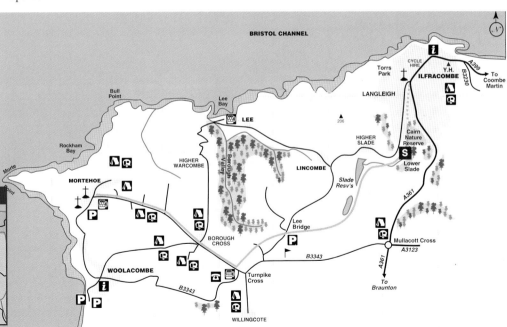

23

PRINCETOWN
Tyrwhitt Cycleway

THE TRAIL IS SITUATED WEST OF PRINCETOWN, EAST OF TAVISTOCK. THE B3357 TAVISTOCK-TWO BRIDGES ROAD TO THE NORTH AND THE BURRATOR RESERVOIR AND B3212 YELVERTON-PRINCETOWN ROAD TO THE SOUTH.

The trail is situated west of Princetown, east of Tavistock. The B3357 Tavistock-Two Bridges road to the north and the Burrator Reservoir and B3212 Yelverton-Princetown road to the South.

This is a very pleasant trail accross the moorland of Walkhampton Common within the Dartmoor National Park. Using the old railway track around King's Tor, passing a couple of disused granite quarries where abandoned 'leftovers' can be seen lying around from when the huge granite blocks were cut out of Swell Tor and Fogginor quarries for building bridges and widening London Bridge in 1903.

This cycle trail was named 'Tyrwhitt Cycleway' to honour Thomas Tyrwhitt who founded Princetown and built the Prison.

The trail begins behind the Fire Station in Princetown, a town having been built from granite quarried nearby, hence its very grey and gloomy appearance.
H.M. Dartmoor Prison was originally built to imprison French prisoners-of-war in the early nineteenth century and is still in use today. the Church of St. Michael is one of the highest churches in England at 420m and was built by the French prisoners plus a few Americans who were imprisoned during the War of Independence.

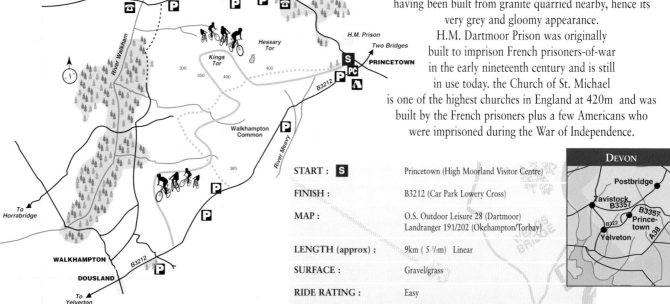

START : ⑤	Princetown (High Moorland Visitor Centre)
FINISH :	B3212 (Car Park Lowery Cross)
MAP :	O.S. Outdoor Leisure 28 (Dartmoor) Landranger 191/202 (Okehampton/Torbay)
LENGTH (approx) :	9km (5 ¹/₂m) Linear
SURFACE :	Gravel/grass
RIDE RATING :	Easy

BARNSTAPLE - BRAUNTON BURROWS

'Tarka Trail'

THE RIDE IS SITUATION ALONG THE NORTH SIDE OF THE RIVER TAW AND SOUTH OF THE A361 BARNSTAPLE - ILFRACOMBE ROAD.

This trail is a continuation of the Tarka trail from Petrockstowe and is very pleasant giving excellent views down the estuary of the River Taw, to the sand dunes on Braunton Burrows. There is a Toll on the road after Velator where a bell rings - but cyclists don't have to pay!

START / FINISH	S	Barnstaple Railway Station
MAP :		O.S. Landranger 180 (Barnstaple & Ilfracombe area)
LENGTH (approx) :		32km (20 m) Circular
SURFACE :		Tarmac/gravel/sand
RIDE RATING :		Easy

NOTE : At Barnstaple railway station follow the cyleway 'Tarka Trail' road signs for Braunton, keeping north of the river.

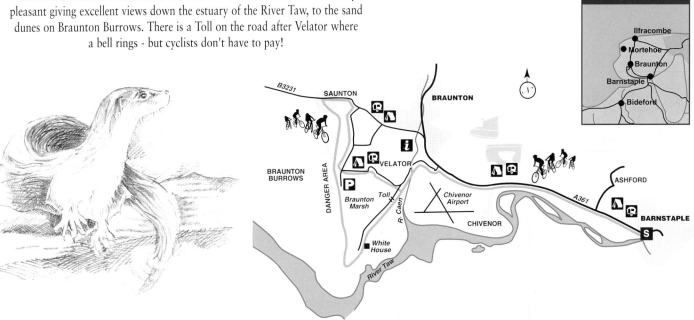

(inset picture) *Ponies beside the East Dart River in Bellever Forest.*

PORTREATH MINERAL TRAMWAY
& Tehidy Country Park

THIS AREA OF CORNWALL IS LITTERED WITH OLD MINE TRAMWAYS. THE PORTREATH TRAIL FOLLOWS ONE OF THE OLD TRAMROADS THROUGH COUNTRYSIDE WHERE THE REMAINS OF OLD BEAM ENGINE HOUSES AND DISUSED MINES CAN BE SEEN. THESE TRAMWAYS WOULD CARRY TIN AND COPPER ORE BETWEEN THE MINES AND THE HARBOUR OF PORTREATH WHERE THE GOODS WOULD BE SHIPPED TO SOUTH WALES AND RETURN WITH COAL TO FUEL THE VAST MINE ENGINES.

Wheal Rose

PORTREATH TRAMWAY

The route of the old tramway is situated between the little port of Portreath on the west coast and the A30 Truro-Penzance road near Scorrier.

The Portreath tramroad began operating in 1812. The tram wagons ran on 3ft long 'L' shaded cast iron plates, usually horse drawn because the plates could not carry the weight of an engine, operating between the copper ore mines of St. Day and Gwennap and Portreath harbour. The tramroad closed in the 1860's when competition became too great from the railways and the last copper ore mine closed.

The route starts out of Portreath (B3300) on a little road opposite the County Primary school. The trail is very clearly signposted and where there is a crossing and no finger sign, keep straight on even though the path of the trail looks smaller than the one your on!

START : **S**		(B3300) Portreath
FINISH :		Scorrier (Plume of Feathers)
MAP :		O.S. Landranger 203/204 (Land's End/Truro, Falmouth area)
LENGTH (approx) :		4 ½km (2 ¾ m) Linear
SURFACE :		Stoney/tarmac
RIDE RATING :		Easy adventurous

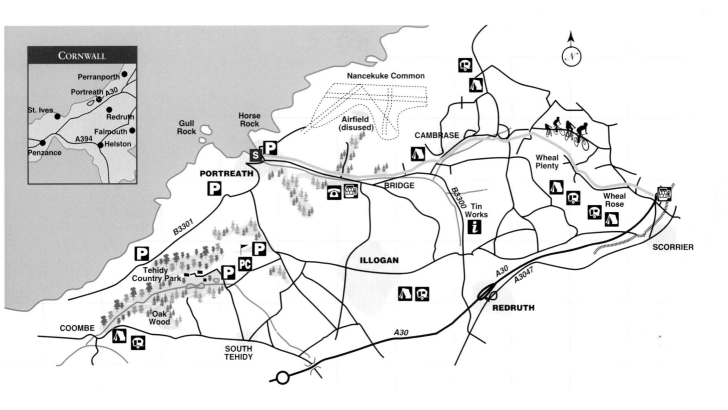

TEHIDY COUNTRY PARK

Start the trail from either the North Cliffe car park off the B3301 Portreath-Hayle road or the South Drive car park taking the road north out of South Tehidy.

The Tehidy Country Park was once part of the estate belonging to the Bassett tin mining family with 250 acres of magnificent woodland.

Within the park there are approximately 6 miles of easy cyling on paths beside the lakes, past Otter Bridge where otters are kept and through very picturesque woods.

PENTEWAN VALLEY

Tʜɪs ᴠᴀʟʟᴇʏ ᴛʀᴀɪʟ ɪs sɪᴛᴜᴀᴛᴇᴅ ɴᴏʀᴛʜ ᴏғ ᴛʜᴇ ᴠɪʟʟᴀɢᴇ ᴏғ Pᴇɴᴛᴇᴡᴀɴ ᴀɴᴅ Mᴇᴠᴀɢɪssᴇʏ Bᴀʏ ᴡɪᴛʜ ᴛʜᴇ B3273 Pᴇɴᴛᴇᴡᴀɴ - Sᴛ Aᴜsᴛᴇʟʟ ʀᴏᴀᴅ ᴛᴏ ᴛʜᴇ ᴡᴇsᴛ.

Pentewan quarried stone was in great demand in the 15th century for rebuilding churches and with the discovery of clay in the 18th century the little port was in constant use, but the harbour is now silted up and no longer any access to the sea.

This very attractive trail was opened in March 1995 and begins beside the river bridge north of Pentewan village. The route follows a path through Woodland Trust land where an abundance of woodland plants can be seen, continuing beside the clear waters of the river which, since the closure of the mines, no longer looks milky white from the clay deposits, and finishes at the London Apprentice.

START : S		Pentewan
FINISH :		London Apprentice
MAP :		O.S. Landranger 204 (Truro & Falmouth area)
LENGTH (approx) :		4 km (2 ½ m) Linear
SURFACE :		Stone based hard core/forest paths
RIDE RATING :		Easy

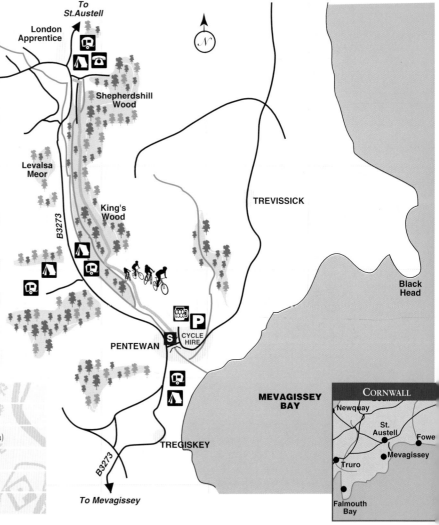

CARDINHAM WOODS

These woods are situated east of Bodmin and the A30(T) road. North of the A38 Bodmin Liskeard road and the village of Turfdown.

Cardinham Woods were acquired by the Forestry Commission in 1922 and extend to 650 acres producing Douglas fir for the British timber industry. There is an abundance of wildlife within the woods including the shy roe and red deer.

This trail has been designed as a very safe off-road route winding its way around the woods on paths with a few gentle climbs. There are plenty of picnic areas and clearings within the woods for seeing the beautiful woodland plants.

Forest Enterprise

START & FINISH : ⬛	Car Park, Cardinham Woods
MAP :	O.S. Landranger 200 (Newquay, Bodmin area)
LENGTH (approx) :	8km (6m) Circular
SURFACE :	Forest tracks/tarmac
RIDE RATING :	Moderate

NOTES : *Follow the cycle trail markers within the woods. Care must be taken as the trail meets the road at Milltown.*

THE CAMEL TRAIL
Padstow - Wadebridge

PADSTOW AND THE CAMEL TRAIL ARE SITUATED EAST OF THE A39(T). TO THE WEST OF THE TRAIL IS PADSTOW BAY. THE A389 IS SOUTH OF THE TRAIL.

The trail follows the south bank of the River Camel along a disused railway track. The river winds through some of Cornwall's most beautiful unspoilt countryside before reaching the very picturesque estuary between Padstow and Rock

The trail starts in the old railway station yard where some of the old siding can still be seen. This railway line to Wadebridge opened in 1899 and became the last addition to North Cornwall's railway. The railway carried thousands of holiday makers 260 miles from Waterloo on the 'Atlantic Coast Express' to Padstow, until its closure in 1967. One of the railways frequent users was the Poet Laureate Sir John Betjeman who lived in Wadebridge.

Sir John is buried north of the Camel Estuary near Rock in the little 13th century church of St. Enodoc which was excavated from the sand in 1863

The Camel Estuary has an abundance of bass and mullet, whilst up river salmon and trout enjoy the clear waters. Heron can frequently be seen along the river bank along with Oystercatchers and flocks of Curlew.

START : S	Padstow, Old Station car park
FINISH :	Wadebridge
MAP :	O.S. Landranger 200 (Newquay, Bodmin)
LENGTH (approx) :	8 km (5 m) Linear
SURFACE :	Stone base/grit
RIDE RATING :	Easy

NOTES : Where the trail does not have a separate cycle lane, pass walkers with care -they have the right of way.

Padstow Harbour.

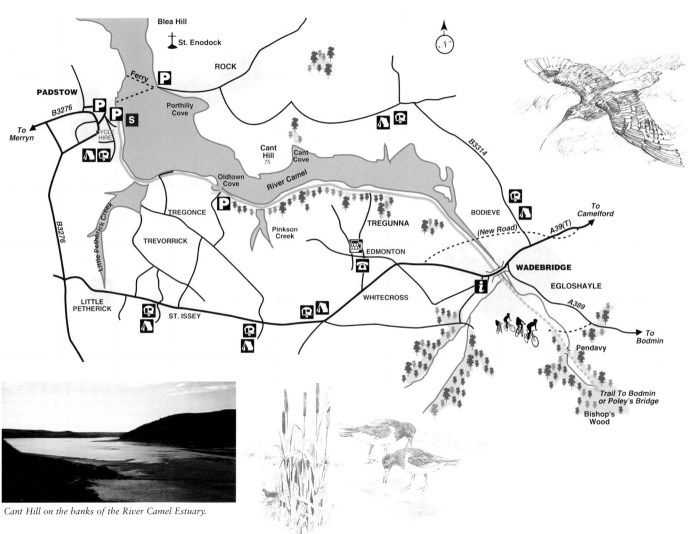

Blea Hill

✝ St. Enodock

ROCK

PADSTOW

Ferry

Porthilly Cove

B3276

To Merryn

CYCLE HIRE

Cant Hill 75

Cant Cove

Oldtown Cove

River Camel

TREGONCE

Little Petherick Creek

Pinkson Creek

TREVORRICK

TREGUNNA

EDMONTON

B3276

BODIEVE

To Camelford

(New Road)

A39(T)

WADEBRIDGE

EGLOSHAYLE

LITTLE PETHERICK

ST. ISSEY

WHITECROSS

A39

B3314

To Bodmin

Pendavy

Trail To Bodmin or Poley's Bridge

Bishop's Wood

Cant Hill on the banks of the River Camel Estuary.

33

THE CAMEL TRAIL
Wadebridge - Poley's Bridge

THE TRAIL IS SITUATION NORTH OF BODMIN AND BETWEEN THE TWO MAJOR ROADS OF
THE A39 ST COLUMB TO CAMELFORD TO THE WEST AND THE A30
LAUNCESTON -TRURO TO THE EAST.

This section of the Camel Trail has two distinct halves, the first half from Wadebridge follows the bed of the old railway line beside the wide banks of the River Camel into Bodmin. The second half from the Bodmin intersection, follows the River Camel as it winds its way through beautiful woodland glades with boughs of the trees touching overhead making tunnels of flickering lights as the sun shines through.

The Cornish Railway linewas taken over by the London and South Western Railway in 1846. The Padstow/Wadebridge section was built in 1899 and ran the Atlantic Coast Express excusions. One of the more popular day trips was to vist Bodmin Gaol to watch the public hangings.

In 1382 Wadebridge was simply called Wade which meant 'ford', and the word 'bridge' was added later. The town now has two bridges, one a beautiful old granite multi-arched and the other a modern bridge carrying the traffic around the town.

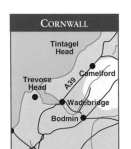

The old Wadebridge railway station has been restored and is now the John Betjeman Centre, housing a collection of photographs and artifacts giving an insight into the poet who loved the Cornish countryside.

Road crossing with the old railway lines still to be seen.

START : **S**		Wadebridge - Jubilee car park
FINISH :		Poley's Bridge
MAP :		O.S. Landranger 200 (Newquay, Bodmin)
LENGTH (approx) :		18 ½ km (11 ½ m) Linear
SURFACE :		Gravel/grit/forest track
RIDE RATING :		Easy

WARNING: At the entrance to the car park at Poley's Bridge there is a head restriction bar of 6ft 3in (1.9m) - just high enough to knock the bikes off your roof!

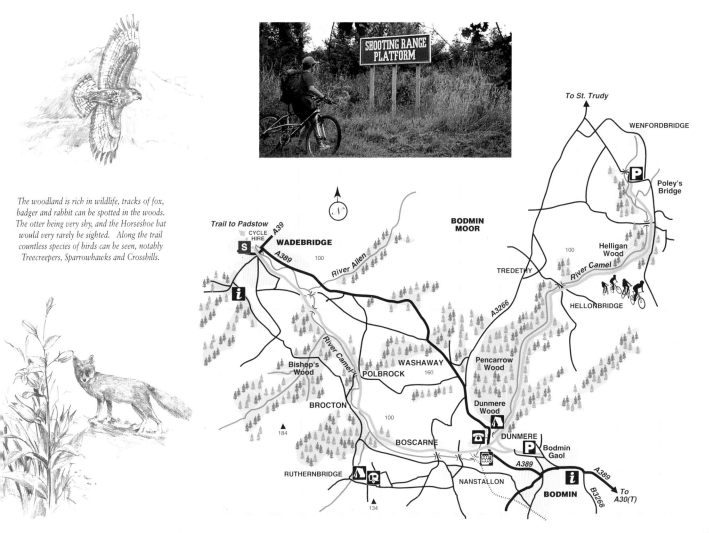

The woodland is rich in wildlife, tracks of fox, badger and rabbit can be spotted in the woods. The otter being very shy, and the Horseshoe bat would very rarely be sighted. Along the trail countless species of birds can be seen, notably Treecreepers, Sparrowhawks and Crossbills.

SHOOTING RANGE PLATFORM

To St. Trudy

WENFORDBRIDGE

Poley's Bridge

BODMIN MOOR

Helligan Wood

TREDETHY

River Camel

100

HELLONBRIDGE

Trail to Padstow

A39

CYCLE HIRE

WADEBRIDGE

A389

100

River Allen

A3266

River Camel

Bishop's Wood

WASHAWAY

Pencarrow Wood

POLBROCK

160

BROCTON

Dunmere Wood

100

DUNMERE

BOSCARNE

Bodmin Gaol

184

A389

RUTHERNBRIDGE

NANSTALLON

BODMIN

A389

B3268

134

To A30(T)

35

BRENDON COMMON
'Doone Country'

THIS ROUTE IS SITUATED IN NORTH EXMOOR, SOUTH OF THE A39 LYNTON TO MINEHEAD ROAD. EAST OF THE B3223 AND WEST OF BADGWORTHY WATER AND OARE COMMON.

The Doone Country trail is a mixture of magnificent views over Exmoor from Withycombe Ridge, the enjoyment of the moorland tracks of Brendon Common and the track along the banks of Badgworthy Water. (memories for those of you who have read the book Lorna Doone.)

The trail begins at Malmsmead, up Post lane, then along the track beside Badgeworthy water. The R.D. Blackmore Memorial stone which commemorates his famous tale of Exmoor and Lorna Doone stands on the bank of the river. Follow the bridleway along Doone Valley, through the oak woods passing Lorna Doone's infamous 'water slide' on the hill to your right. The trail continues through the wood until you reach the bridleway sign for Brendon Common on your right.

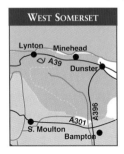

WEST SOMERSET

Keeping Badgworthy hill on your left hand side the open moorland track climbs towards Brendon Common and Withycombe Ridge. Keep on the bridleway tracks over the moorland to Easter/Post lane before returning to Malmsmead. Any energy left - the track through Southern Wood is well worth a detour before returning to the Lorna Doone Farm and the tea shop.

Lorna Done Farm at Malmsmead beside the ford over Badgworthy water.

START & FINISH :	**S**	Malmsmead
MAP :		O.S. Landranger 180 (Barnstaple & Ilfracombe area) Outdoor Leisure 9 (Exmoor)
LENGTH (approx) :		15km (9 ½ m) Circular
SURFACE :		Moorland/gravel
RIDE RATING :		Hard Adventurous

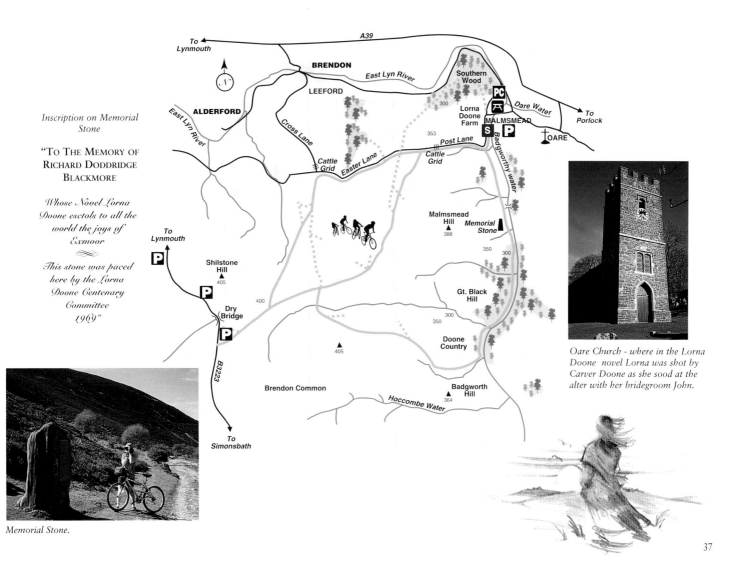

A39

To Lynmouth

BRENDON

East Lyn River

Southern Wood

PC

Dare Water

To Porlock

LEEFORD

300

Lorna Doone Farm

MALMSMEAD

ALDERFORD

East Lyn River

Cross Lane

S **P**

OARE

353

Post Lane

Cattle Grid

Easter Lane

Cattle Grid

Badgworthy water

Malmsmead Hill
388

Memorial Stone

350 300

To Lynmouth

P

Shilstone Hill
405

P

400

Gt. Black Hill

350 300

Dry Bridge

P

405

Doone Country

B3223

Brendon Common

Badgworth Hill
364

Hoccombe Water

To Simonsbath

Inscription on Memorial Stone

"To The Memory of Richard Doddridge Blackmore

Whose Novel Lorna Doone esctols to all the world the joys of Exmoor

This stone was paced here by the Lorna Doone Centenary Committee 1969"

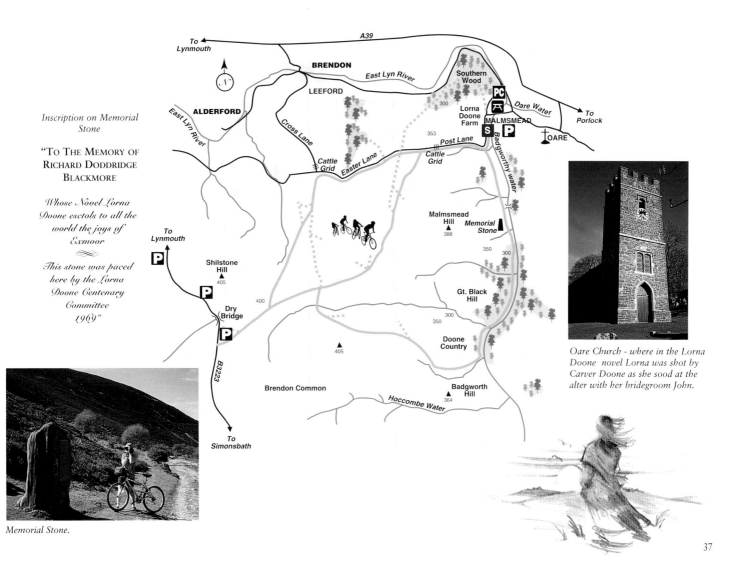

Memorial Stone.

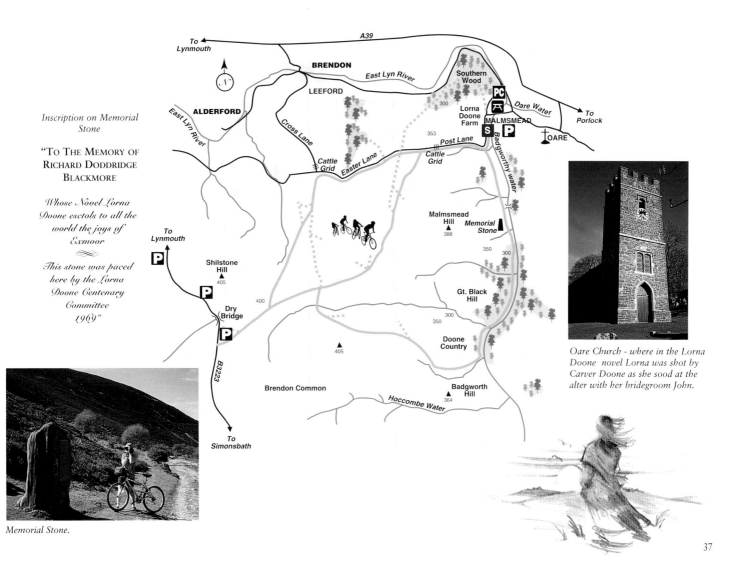

Oare Church - where in the Lorna Doone novel Lorna was shot by Carver Doone as she sood at the alter with her bridegroom John.

DUNSTER PARK & CROYDON HILL

THE TRAILS ARE WITHIN THE CROWN ESTATE FOREST SOUTH OF DUNSTER WITHIN EXMOOR NATIONAL PARK. TO THE WEST IS THE A396 FROM DUNSTER TO WHEDDON CROSS AND TO THE EAST THE A39 FROM DUNSTER TO WASHFORD.

The trails are within the Crown Estate forest south of Dunster within Exmoor National Park. To the west is the A396 from Dunster to Wheddon Cross and to the east the A39 from Dunster to Washford.

These two trails are wonderful forest routes, both having fairly steep but easily negotiable hills. From the route going up Croydon Hill there are magnificent views of the hills of West Somerset.

Route 1 Keeping your feet dry is your first task as you negotiate the ford before ascending Vinegar Hill. The trail beside the stream through King's Head Coppice does get muddy after a rainy spell, but once past the footbridge on your right there is a good hard gravel track taking you down the hill, round Dunster Park and back to the ford.

Route 2 Take a left hand turn out of the car park going up the road towards Croydon Hill. Turn left at the first major bridleway crossing, follow the forest track up the hill keeping Croydon Hill on your right. The bridleway trails are very clearly marked on the forest paths. Having turned onto the bridleway beside the clearing of Withycombe Common there is a two mile down hill ride taking you through King's Hedge Coppice and back on to the forest road. Turn left for the car park and picnic area.

WEST SOMERSET

Track alongside the forest beside Black Hill.

START &	**S¹**	Gallox Bridge Car Park
FINISH	**S²**	Nutcombe Bottom Picnic area
MAP :		O.S. Landranger 181 (Minehead & Brendon Hills area) Outdoor Leisure 9 (Exmoor)
LENGTH (approx) :		Route 1 6 km (3 ¾m) Circular Route 2 8km (5m) Circular
SURFACE :		Both routes : Forest tracks/tarmac
RIDE RATING :		Route 1 Moderate Route 2 Hard

NOTE : *This is a working forest and care must be taken to follow all warning signs where ever timber harvesting is in operation.*

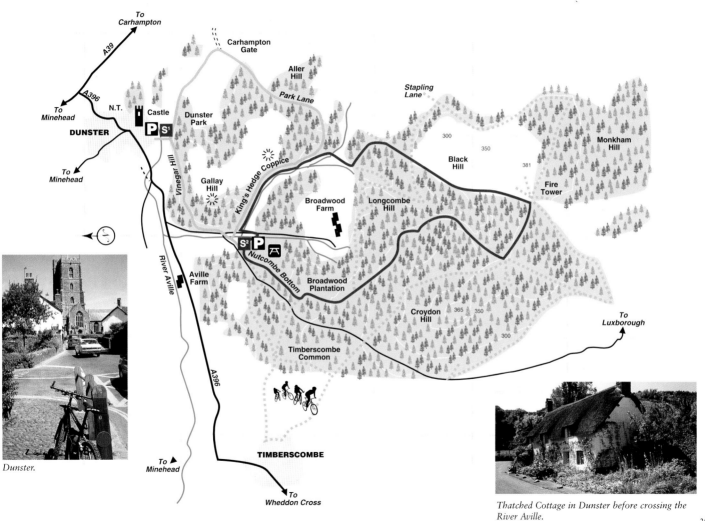

To Carhampton

A39

A396

To Minehead

N.T.

To Minehead

DUNSTER

Castle

P S¹

Carhampton Gate

Aller Hill

Park Lane

Dunster Park

Stapling Lane

300

350

Black Hill

381

Monkham Hill

Fire Tower

Vinegar Hill

Gallay Hill

King's Hedge Coppice

Broadwood Farm

Longcombe Hill

River Aville

S² P

Nutcombe Bottom

Aville Farm

Broadwood Plantation

Croydon Hill

365 350

300

To Luxborough

A396

Timberscombe Common

TIMBERSCOMBE

To Minehead

To Wheddon Cross

Dunster.

Thatched Cottage in Dunster before crossing the River Aville.

39

BRIDGWATER & TAUNTON CANAL

THE CANAL FLOWS BETWEEN THE TOWNS OF TAUNTON AND BRIDGWATER WITH THE M5 TO THE WEST AND THE RIVERS TONE AND PARRETT TO THE EAST.

The Bridgwater to Taunton Canal is a very quite and peaceful waterway going through some beautiful unspoilt countryside full of wildlife. The canal was opened in 1827 and was part of a scheme proposed to link the Bristol Channel with the English Channel, but due to the growing popularity of the railway, was never completed.

Once the fifth largest port on Britain, Bridgwater also built docks on the River Parrett, completed in 1841, as safe shelter for the ships undergoing repair.

Trail along the Bridgwater and Taunton Canal.

Cromwell's famous 'General at Sea', Admiral Robert Blake came from Bridgwater. As a consequence of his gaining many battle honours at sea in the Mediterranean and the West Indies and also for bettering the welfare of the sailors, he was the first sealord to have a grand funeral at Westminster Abbey.

The trail commences half-way between Bridgwater and Taunton on the towpath of the canal at Lower Maunsel Lock, giving two circular rides of 14 miles in each direction with an opportunity of having a break on the middle of you route at the old Lock Keeper's cottage cafe at Lower Maunsel.

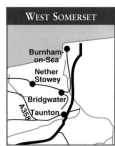

The trail can be continued from Creech St. Michael for a further 1 1/2 miles, where it finishes at the Coal Orchard car park in the centre of Taunton.

START & FINISH : S	(Off the A38 sign posted "canal car park") Lower Maunsel Lock
MAP :	O.S. Landranger 182 (Weston-super-Mare & Bridgwater area) Landranger 193 (Taunton & Lyme Regis)
LENGTH (approx) :	22 1/2km (14m) Linear (Bridgwater - Taunton)
SURFACE :	Grass/hardcore/tarmac
RIDE RATING :	Easy

NOTES : A cycle permit is required - obtainable from Maunsel Canal Centre, Maunsel Lock Cottage, Banklands, North Newton, Bridgwater, Somerset TA7 0DH (Tel: 01278 663160).

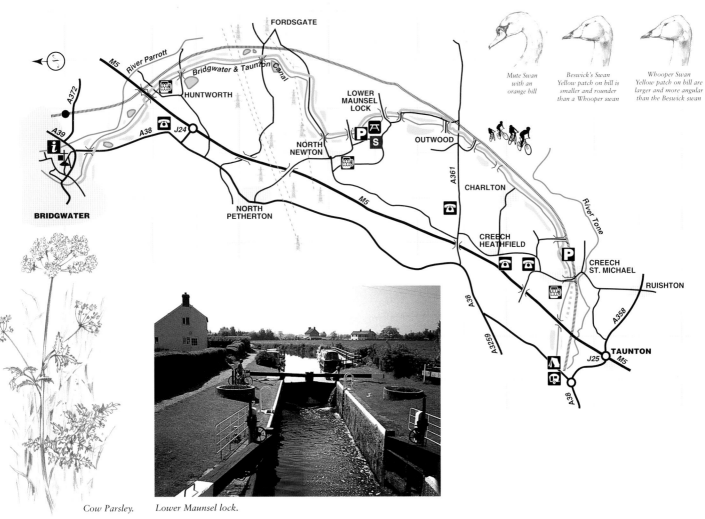

FORDSGATE

River Parrott

M5

A372

A39

Bridgwater & Taunton Canal

HUNTWORTH

A38

J24

BRIDGWATER

NORTH NEWTON

NORTH PETHERTON

M5

LOWER MAUNSEL LOCK

OUTWOOD

A361

CHARLTON

CREECH HEATHFIELD

CREECH ST. MICHAEL

RUISHTON

A358

River Tone

A38

A3259

J25

TAUNTON

M5

A38

Mute Swan
with an
orange bill

Beswick's Swan
Yellow patch on bill is
smaller and rounder
than a Whooper swan

Whooper Swan
Yellow patch on bill are
larger and more angular
than the Beswick swan

Cow Parsley. Lower Maunsel lock.

QUANTOCK HILLS

THESE HILLS ARE SITUATED EAST OF EXMOOR NEAR THE COAST. BETWEEN THE A358 WILLITON TO TAUNTON ROAD AND A39 ROUTE FROM MINEHEAD TO BRIDGWATER.

These hills are situated east of Exmoor near the coast. Between the A358 Williton to Taunton road and A39 route from Minehead to Bridgwater.

The Quantocks are a very attractive range of hills partially wooded with a fine ridge running between the Lydeard hill and the summit of Beacon Hill with some exceptional views over the surrounding area. The village of Nether Stowey on route 2 was the home of Samuel Taylor Coleridge who composed such classics as the 'Rime of the Ancient Mariner'. Coleridge often walked through this area of Devon with his friend William Wordsworth who lived nearby at Alfoxton Park, now a hotel.

Route 1 ▬▬ is an old drover's road traversing the length of the ridge between Lydeard Hill and Beacon Hill. Although the track is gritty with a a couple of climbs the views over Exmoor and the Brendon hills are breathtaking.

Once past Wills Neck and the Park gates of Crowcombe the trail takes you past a trig point at 358m (1,174ft) overlooking Dowsborough Hill Fort. The trail continues to a very lonely sign at Bicknoller Post giving directions to West Quantoxhead, Perry Farm and Holford, before the path to the summit of Beacon Hill. It is well worth walking up to the summit as the views of the coast and the Bristol Channel are exceptional.

Route 2 ▬▬ begins with a steep descent into Nether Stowey then a climb up Nether Stowey Lane into the forests past Great Bear summit. After the C.P. at 'Dead Woman's Ditch' carry on up the lane to the gates of Crowcombe Park turn right to return to Lydeard Hill C.P. or left going down the bridleway of Black Hill to the village of Holford. (Longstone Hill is a very steep climb to Bicknoller Post, you may prefer when at the park gates to ride along the ridge to Bicknoller Post and descend Longstone Hill returning up Black Hill bridleway) Return along the drove road to Lydeard Hill.

START & FINISH 1 & 2 : **S**	Lydeard Hill Car Park	
MAP :	O.S. Landranger 181 (Minehead & Brendon Hills area)	
LENGTH (approx) :	Route 1 18km (11m) Circular	
	Route 2 28km (17 1/2m) Circular	
SURFACE :	Gravel	
RIDE RATING :	Route 1 Moderate Adventurous	
	Route 2 Hard Adventurous	

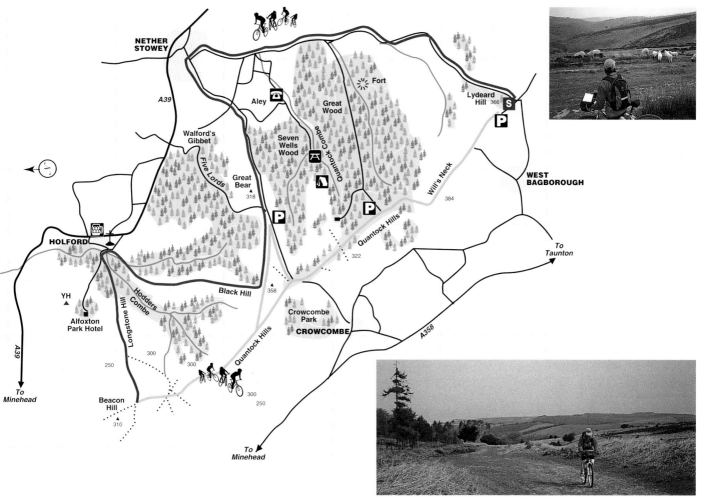

NETHER STOWEY

A39

Aley

Walford's Gibbet

Five Lords

Great Bear
▲ 318

Seven Wells Wood

Quantock Combe

Great Wood

Fort

Lydeard Hill 366
S
P

WEST BAGBOROUGH

Will's Neck
384

Quantock Hills
322

HOLFORD

YH
▲

Alfoxton Park Hotel

Hodders Combe

Longstone Hill

Black Hill

▲ 358

Quantock Hills

Crowcombe Park

CROWCOMBE

A358

To Taunton

A39

To Minehead

300

250

300

300

250

Beacon Hill
⋮ 310

To Minehead

Beacon Hill.

43

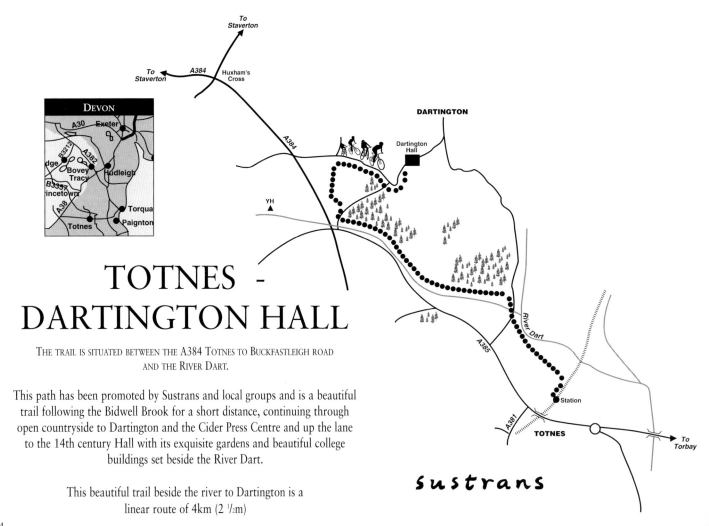

TOTNES - DARTINGTON HALL

THE TRAIL IS SITUATED BETWEEN THE A384 TOTNES TO BUCKFASTLEIGH ROAD
AND THE RIVER DART.

This path has been promoted by Sustrans and local groups and is a beautiful
trail following the Bidwell Brook for a short distance, continuing through
open countryside to Dartington and the Cider Press Centre and up the lane
to the 14th century Hall with its exquisite gardens and beautiful college
buildings set beside the River Dart.

This beautiful trail beside the river to Dartington is a
linear route of 4km (2 ½m)

EXETER SHIP CANAL TRAIL

The Canal was built in the 1700's for large trading ships, now used mainly for leisure craft This cycle route begins on the Quay beside the River Exe. Take the cycle route over the Blue suspension bridge and turn left. Follow the path along the River Exe. Turn left over the Exeter Ship Canal and continue through the Riverside Valley Park where kingfishers and herons can be frequently seen. Take the first trail on the right and cycle to the bridge. Turn left down the road to the Double Locks on the Exeter Ship Canal.

This trail beside the Canal is a leisurely, flat and very easy linear route of 4 ¾ km (3 m)

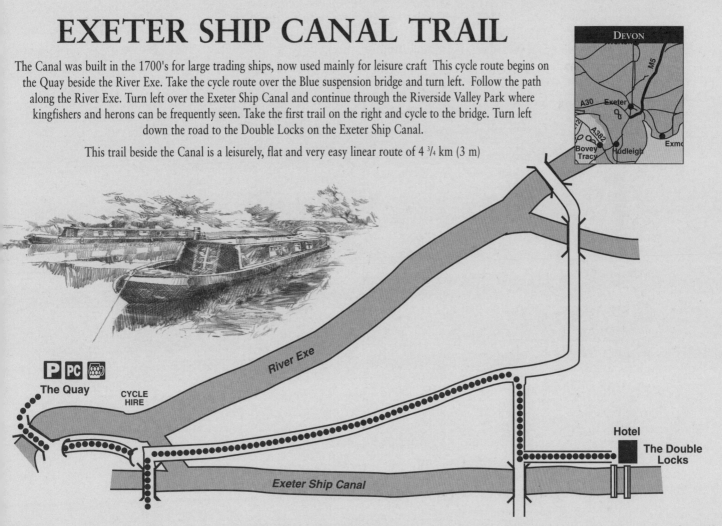

DEVON

M5

A30   Exeter

A382

Bovey   Hdleigh   Exmo
Tracy

P PC

The Quay

CYCLE
HIRE

River Exe

Exeter Ship Canal

Hotel

**The Double
Locks**

CYCLE HIRE CENTRES

The following is a list of cycle hire centres. Intending hirers should telephone for opening times and types of bikes available.

DEVON

Tarka Trail Cycle Hire
Barnstaple Rail Station
BARNSTAPLE
Tel: 01271 24202

Otter Cycle Hire
Station Road
BRAUNTON
Tel: 01271 813339

East Devon Cycle Hire
Knowle Hill
BUDLEIGH SALTERTON
Tel: 01395 446484

Eggesford Cycle Hire
Eddesford Forest
CHULMLEIGH
Tel: 01759 580250

Bideford Cycle Hire
Torrington Street
EAST-THE-WATER
Nr. Bideford
Tel: 01237 424123

Saddles & Paddles
4 Kings Wharfe
The Quay
EXETER
Tel: 01392 424241
Partridge Cycles
Gissons House
KENNFORD
Nr. Exeter
Tel: 01392 832289

Okehampton Cycle Centre
Bostock garden Centre
North Roach
OKEHAMPTON
Tel: 01837 53248

Tavistock Cycles Mtn Bike Hire
Paddons Row
Brook Street
TAVISTOCK
Tel: 01822 617630

Mylor Cycles
10 Northumberland Place
TEIGNMOUTH
Tel: 01626 778460

Maynards Cycle Shop
25 Gold Street
TIVERTON
Tel: 01884 253979

Torrington Cycle Hire
Unit 1, Station Yard
TORRINGTON
Tel: 01805 622633

Yelland Cycle Hire
Estury Ind. Park
WEST YELLAND
Nr. Barnstaple
Tel: 01271 861424

CORNWALL

Glenn Valley Cycle Hire
(Sundays/Bank Hols)
Cardinham Woods
Margate
BODMIN
Tel: 01208 74244

Bike Shop
25 Honey Street
Church Square
BODMIN
Tel: 01208 72557

North Coast Cycles
Flexbury Garage
Ocean View road
BUDE
Tel: 01288 352974

Moorland Cycle Hire
Hallagenna Farm
St. Breward
BODMIN MOOR
Nr. Bodmin
Tel: 01208 850439
Altridge Cycles
38 Cross Street
CAMBOURNE
Tel: 01209 714970

Penwith Cycles
FALMOUTH
Tel: 01326 319412

Liskeard Cycles
(Summer only)
Pig Meadow Lane
LISKEARD
Tel: 01579

Cycle Revolution
7 Beach Road
NEWQUAY
Tel: 01637 872364

Silly Cycles
The Shop
Wesley Yard
NEWQUAY
01637 872455

Glyn Davies Hire
Unit 6
South Quay
PADSTOW
Tel: 01841 532594

Wheels Cycle Shop
3 Red House Shopping Centre
Boscawen road
PERRANPORTH
Tel:

Pentewan Bicycle Hire
West End
PENTEWAN
Nr. St. Austell
Tel: 01726 844242

Geoff's Bikes
Victoria Place
PENZANCE
Tel: 01736 363665

Bike Chain
82 Mount Ambrose
REDRUTH
Tel: 01209 212100

Truro Cycles
110 Kenwyn Street
TRURO
Tel: 01872 271703

Bridge Bike Hire
(Camel Trail)
Eddystone Road
WADEBRIDGE
Tel: 01208 813050

Park & Ride
Savers Supermarket
Eddystone Road
WADEBRIDGE
Tel: 01208 814303

ACCOMMODATION GUIDE

For further information on accommodation contact the Information Centres, Telephone numbers on page 50.

NORTH DEVON - EXMOOR

BARNSTAPLE	Netherne ,Clogshill Cross, Yarnscombe,	01271 858297
	Jackie Payne, Huxtahle Farm, West Buckland	01598 760254
	Susan Blake, Rock Villa, Brayford	01598 710782
	Hazel Kingdon, Waytown Farm, Shirwell	01271 850396
BIDEFORD	Julia Carter, Burnards, Weare Giffard	01237 473809
	Eleanor Curtis, Bracken Haven, Weare Giffard	01237 472918
	Sunset Hotel, Landcross	01237 472962
BRAUNTON	Preston House Hotel, Saunton	01271 890472
CHALLACOMBE	Helen Asher,Twitchen Farm	01598763568
CHUMLEIGH	Mrs Crocombe, Parsonage Farm	01769 580420
ILFRACOMBE	Epchris Hotel, Torrs Park	01271 862 751
	Sunnymead Country House Hotel,West Down	01271 863668
LYNTON	Rodwell, 21 Lee Road	01598 753324
	South Cheriton Farm, Cheriton	01598 753280
NORTH TAWTON	Lower Nychols Nymet Farm, Lwr Nychols Nymet	01363 82510
	Kayden House Hotel, High Street	01837 82242
SOUTH MOULTON	West Trayne, Phyl Rawle, Georgenympton	01769 572534

TORRINGTON	Ann Smith the Roundhouse, Guscott,	
	Huntshaw Water	01271 858626
	Black Horse Inn, High Street	01805 622121
UMBERLEIGH	Sally Hunt, Cleave Farm, Burrington	01769 53239
	The Gables, On The Bridge	01769 560461
WOOLACOMBE	The Waters Fall Hotel, Beach Road	01271 870365

WEST & SOUTH DEVON - DARTMOOR

BOVEY TRACEY	Front House Lodge, East Street	01626 832202
BRIDFORD	Bridford Guest House, nr. Exeter	01647 252563
BUCKFASTLEIGH	Filbury Manor Farm, Coston road	01364 644079
CHAGFORD	Yellam Country House, Yellam	01647 432211
CHERITON BISHOP	Mrs Nola Stephens, Horselake Farm,	01647 24220
	The Old Thatch Inn	01647 24204
DREWSTEIGNTON	Old Inn Restaurant, 2 The Square	01647 281276
EXETER	Moor Farm, Dunsford	01647 24292
	Hill Farm, Dittisleigh	01647 24149
HATHERLEIGH	Higher Cadham Farm, Jacobstowe	01837 851647
	The Bridge Inn, Bridge Street	01837 810947
	George Hotel, Market Street	01837 810454
IVYBRIDGE	Hillhead Farm, Ughborough	01752 892674

ACCOMMODATION GUIDE

OKEHAMPTON	Bourna Farm House, Huish, Merton	01805 804584
	Christine Heard, Friars Hele, Meeth	01837 810282
	Mrs Watson, Tawside House, Sticklepath	01837840183
	Knowle Farm, Bridestowe	01837 861241
	Nigel Millett, The Tors, Belstone	01837 840689
	Mrs A. Crocker, Heathergate, Lydford	01822 820486
	Old Vicarage Farm, Broadmoor Lane	01837 52559
MORETON-HAMPSTEAD	Judith Harvey, Budleigh Farm	01647 440835
	Cookshayes Country Guest House, Court Street	01647 440374
	Great Sloncombe Farm	01647 440595
NEWTON ABBOT	New Cott Farm, Poundsgate	01364 631421
	Sue Gifford, Wellpritton Farm, Holne	01364 631273
NORTH BOVEY	Gate House, The Village	01647 440479
POSTBRIDGE	Higher Lydgate Farm	01822 880274
	Lydgate House Hotel	01822 880209
PRINCETOWN	Duchy House, Tavistock Road	01822 890552
TAVISTOCK	April Cottage, Mount Tavy Road	01822 613280
	New Court Farm, Lamerton	01822 614319
	Colcharton Farm, Gulworthy	01822 616435
THROWLEIGH	Well Farm	01647 231294
YELVERTON	Eggworthy Farm, Sampford Spiney	01822 852142
	Withill Farm, Sampford Spiney	01822 853992
	Mrs A Wing, Rosehill, Clearbrook	01822 852130
	The Forge, Clearbrook House, Clearbrook	01822 853386
WINKLEIGH	Middlecott Farm, Broadwoodkelly	01837 83381

CORNWALL

CALLINGTON	East Cornwall Farmhouse, Fullaford Road	01579 350018
CAMELFORD	Lanteglos Hotel & Villas,	01840 213551
CAWSAND	Mrs. Fidler, Rame Barton Guest House, Rame	01752 822789
LISKEARD	Tresulgan Farm, Nr. Menheniot	01579 383010
	Colliford Tavern, Colliford Lake St. Neot	01208 821335
	Higher Trevartha Farm, Pengover	01579 343382
	Trewint Farm, Menheniot	01579 347155
LOOE	Westcliffe Guest Houses, West Road	01503 262927
	Schooner Point Guest House, Polperro Road	01503 262670
	Trisha Todd, Little Mainstone	01503 262983
NEWQUAY	Trevelgue Hotel, Porth	01637 872864
	The Rosemere Hotel, Watergate Bay	01637 860238
PADSTOW	Lesley Mills,	01841 533161
POLPERRO	Lanhael House, Langreek Road	01503 272428
	Crumplehorn Inn,	01503 272348
	Mrs Hitchman, The Wildings Tallard Hill	01503 272452
	Little Tregue, Langreek Road	01503 272758
PORT ISSAC	Trentinney Farm	01208 880564
SALTASH	Weary Friar Inn, Pillaton	01579 350238
TORPOINT	Kathy Ridpath, Fir Cottage	01752 822626
	Mrs. S. Blake, Stone Farm Whitsand Bay	01752 822267
WADEBRIDGE	The Olde House, Chapel Amble	01208 813219
	Molesworth Arms Hotel	01208 812055

YOUTH HOSTELS

BELLEVER	Postbridge Telverton Devon	01822880302
BOSCASTLE HARBOUR	Palace Stables, Cornwall	01840 250287
BOSWINGER	St. Austell, Cornwall	01726 843234
CHEDDAR	Hillfield, Somerset	01934 742494
CROWCOMBE HEATHFIELD	Densel House, Taunton, Somerset	01984 667249
DARTINGTON	Lownard, Totnes, Devon	01803 862303
ELMSCOTT	Hartland, Bideford, Devon	01237 441367
EXFORD	Exe Mead, Minehead, Somerset	01643 831288
GOLANT	Penquite House, Fowey, Cornwall	01726 833507
ILLFRACOMBE	Ashmour House, Hilsborough Terrace, Devon	01271 865337
INSTOW	Worlington House, New Road, Devon	01271 860394
LAND'S END	Letcha Vean, St. Just-in-Penwith, Cornwall	01736 788437
LYNTON	Lynbridge, Devon	01598 753237
MAYPOOL	Haypool House, Galmpton, Brixham, Devon	01803 842444
MINEHEAD	Alcombe Combe, Somerset	01643 702595
PENDENNIS CASTLE	Falmouth, Cornwall	01326 311435
PERRANPORTH	Droskyn Point, Cornwall	01872 573812
PLYMOUTH	Blemont House, Stoke, Devon	01752 562189
QUANTOCK HILLS	Sevenacres, Holford, Bridgwater, Somerset	01278 741224
SALCOMBE	Overbecks, Sharpitor, Devon	01548 842856
STEPS BRIDGE	Dunsford, Exeter, Devon	01647 252435
STREET	The Chalet, Ivythorne Hill, Somerset	01458 442961
TINTAGEL	Dunderhole Point, Cornwall	01840 770334
TREYARNON-BAY	Tregonnan, Treyarnon, Padstow, Cornwall	01841 520322

yha

Send for Other GUIDES in The Series

BUY TWO AND GET 20% DISCOUNT

20% OFF

COVERING LEISURE CYCLE ROUTES IN

Derbyshire, Peak National Park and Cheshire

Lancashire and the Lake District

Yorkshire Dales, Humberside, North and West Yorkshire

Please send me the following Wilde's Guides:

☐ Copies of Derbyshire, Peak National Park and Cheshire @ £6.75

☐ Copies of Lancashire and the Lake District @ £6.75

☐ Copies of Yorkshire Dales, North Yorkshire and Humberside @ £7.50

☐ Copies of Devon, Cornwall and West Somerset @ £7.95

Total Cost: ....

Name:..

Address:..

Postcode:................

Payment: Credit Card ☐   Cheque* ☐   Postal Order ☐

Credit Card ☐☐☐☐ ☐☐☐☐ ☐☐☐☐ ☐☐☐☐

Expiry Date ☐☐ ☐☐

Signature:..........................

WILDE'S

*Please make cheques payable to Gildersleve Publishing Ltd *(Allow 28 days for delivery)*
Post with Payment to: Gildersleve Publishing, Capricorn House, Rising Bridge, Lancashire BB5 2AA.

TOURIST INFORMATION CENTRES

For further cycle hire and accommodation please contact the following centres.

BARNSTAPLE	01271 388483
BIDEFORD	01237 477676
BODMIN	01208 76616
BRAUNTON	01271 816400
COMBE MARTIN	01271 883319
EXETER	01392 265700
LYNTON	01598 752225
MINEHEAD	01643 702624
MORTEHOE	01271 870553
OKEHAMPTON	01837 53020
PLYMOUTH	01752 264849
PADSTOW	01841 533449
PERRANPORTH	01872 573368
PRINCETOWN	01822 89414
ST. AUSTELL	01726 76333
TAUNTON	01823 274785
TOTNES	01803 863168
WADEBRIDGE	01208 813725
YEOVIL	01935 71279

NOTES

LIFE EDUCATION CENTRES

The first Life Education Centre was established in Australia by the Rev Ted Noffs in 1976.
He had been counselling drug abusers for ten years when he decided that a more proactive approach
to the drug problem was needed.

Most work in the field of drug abuse deals with treatment - in a sense trying to 'cure' the problem after it has arisen. Ted's innovation was to begin at the beginning. He wanted to prevent the problem by educating children before they started taking drugs.

The idea was first brought to Britain in 1986, stimulated by HRH The Prince of Wales' interest and the recognition that this country needed a similar solution to a growing problem.

Over 300,000 British children presently participate in the programme.
There are now over 100 mobile classrooms throughout the world, involving some three million children.

THE REGISTERED CHARITY

Effective drug education cannot be left until adolescence. Life Education Centres offer preventive drug abuse programmes for children from three to 15 years of age. These programmes aim to educate children about the positive aspects of being alive and relate

to all form of drugs, both legal and illegal. They are aimed at providing children with an awareness of themselves by getting to know the incredible functions of the human body, particularly how and why its delicate equilibrium is affected by substances.

Life Education Centres also offers HIV prevention programmes for children from nine to 15 years old, as well as programmes for parents and teachers.

PLEASE HELP LIFE EDUCATION CENTRES AND THEIR DRUG PREVENTION PROGRAMMES FOR CHILDREN.

METHODS

Life Education is a totally positive approach. The graded programmes aim to develop decision making skills, build self esteem and develop a variety of skills necessary for the fulfilment of an individual's full potential.

Life Education Centres for Lancashire is one of more than 20 regional groups. The Group has raised funds for two mobile learning centres, built at a cost of £80,000 each, with running costs of £30,000 for each unit, each year. LEC Lancashire's goal is to purchase six units by the year 2000.

Your contribution will be used towards purchasing new mobile classrooms. If you can make a donation, please be generous and in particular, consider making a regular commitment of a few pounds each month to provide an income we can rely on.

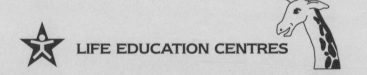

LIFE EDUCATION CENTRES

John Ward, Company Secretary, c/o Roscoe Lynn, 8, 9, & 10 Walton's Parade, Preston, Lancs PR1 3JX.
Registered Charity No 1058867
Company Limited by Guarantee No 03264870

Yes I'll help

NAME ....

ADDRESS ....

....

POSTCODE .... PHONE ....

[ ] Please send information about Life Education Centres.

EITHER

YES I'll help with a donation of:
[£15] [£25] [£50] [£100] [£ ____ other] (please tick)

Please EITHER enclose cheque/PO payable to Life Education Centres for Lancashire or complete your Access/Visa No. here and sign:

Card Expiry Date ....

Signature .... Date ....

———————— / ———— —+— —+—

AND/OR

Help with a monthly standing order of:
[£3] [£5] [£10] [£15] [£25]
[£_____other] (please tick)

NAME OF MY BANK ....

ADDRESS OF MY BANK ....

Current Acc No _ _/_ _/_ _/_ _/_ _/_ _/_ _/_ _/

Bank Sort Code _ _/_ _/-_ _/_ _/-_ _/_ _/

MY NAME ....

Signature .... Date ....

PLEASE DON'T FORGET TO COMPLETE YOUR OWN ADDRESS ABOVE!
Remember. You can cancel this standing order at any time by informing your bank

BANK INSTRUCTION: Please pay the above sum on the 1st next and monthly thereafter to Life Education Centres, Acc. No 25482661 Nat West, 28 bank Street Rawtenstall, Rossendale Lancashire BB4 8D2. Sort Code 01-0729

Please post to Life Education Centres, 'Malolos', 7 Towneley Close, Lancaster LA1 5UX

Thank you